J. R. R. Tolkien's

# THE HOBBIT

## Student Guide

MEMORIA PRESS

www.MemoriaPress.com

J. R. R. Tolkien's
THE HOBBIT

STUDENT GUIDE

Contributing Editors: Cheryl Lowe, Brett Vaden, Sean Brooks

ISBN 978-1-61538-064-0



Cover Illustration: Daniel Young

# Contents

## The Hobbit



## Appendix

## PREPARING TO READ:

### REVIEW

- Orally review any previous vocabulary.
- Review the plot of the book as read so far.
- Periodically review the concepts of character, setting, and plot.

### STUDY GUIDE PREVIEW

- Reading Notes:
  - Read aloud together.
  - This section gives the student key characters, places, and terms that are relevant to a particular time period, etc.
- Vocabulary:
  - Read aloud together so that students will recognize words when they come across them in their reading.
  - Look at each word within the context that it is used, and help your student come up with the best synonym that defines the word. (Make sure it is a synonym the student knows the meaning of.)
  - Record the word's meaning in the students' study guides. (Use students' knowledge of Latin and other vocabulary to decipher meanings.)
- Comprehension Questions:
  - Read through these questions with students to encourage purposeful reading.

## READING:

- Student reads the chapter (or selection of the chapter for that lesson) independently or to the teacher (for younger students).
- For younger students, you can alternate between teacher-read and student-read passages. Model good reading skills. Encourage students to read expressively and smoothly. The teacher may occasionally take oral reading grades.
- While reading, mark each vocabulary word as you come across it.
- Have students take note in their study guide margin of pages where a Comprehension Question is answered.

## AFTER READING:

### COMPREHENSION QUESTIONS

- Older students can answer these questions independently, but younger students (2nd-4th) need to answer the questions orally, form a good sentence, and then write it down, using correct punctuation, capitalization, and spelling. (You may want to write the sentence down for the younger student after forming it orally, and then let the student copy it perfectly.)
- It is not necessary to write the answer to every question; some may be better answered orally. Just make sure you answer the questions that will appear on tests so that students will have the information they need to study.
- Answering questions and composing answers is a valuable learning activity. Questions require students to think; writing a concise answer is a good composition exercise.

## QUOTATIONS AND DISCUSSION QUESTIONS

- Use the Quotations and Discussion Questions section of each lesson as a guide to your oral discussion of the key concepts in the chapter that may not be covered in the comprehension questions.
- These talking points can take your oral discussion to a higher level than covered in the students' written work. Use this time as an opportunity to introduce higher-level thinking. You can introduce concepts the students may not be mature enough to fully understand yet but that would be beneficial for them to begin thinking about.
- A key to the Discussion Questions is in the back of the Teacher Guide.

## ENRICHMENT

- The Enrichment activities include composition, copywork, dictation, research, mapping, drawing, poetry work, literary terms, and more.
- This section has a variety of activities in it, but the most valuable activity is composition. Your student should complete at least one composition assignment each week. Proof student's work and have student copy composition until grammatically perfect. Insist on clear, concise writing. For younger students, start with 2-3 sentences, and do the assignment together. The student can form good sentences orally as you write them down, and then the student copies them.
- These activities can be completed as time and interest allow. Do not feel you need to complete all of these activities. Choose the ones that you feel are the best use of your students' time.

## UNIT REVIEW AND TESTS

- There is a unit review and a quiz or test following every few lessons (varies by individual guide).
- On the weeks that have these reviews and tests, you may want to do the review early in the week, and then drill it orally a couple of times before giving the test at the end of the week.
- A final comprehensive test is also included.

John Ronald Reuel Tolkien lived from 1892 until 1973. His lifetime included the rise of the automobile and motion pictures, World Wars I and II, the discovery of atomic energy, the beginning of space exploration, and the first computers. John Ronald, however, was not as attracted to the new world of machines and technology as he was to an older world—the world that contained the English countryside where he grew up, the world that held the stories and myths he loved to read (and write) about, and the world of simple things he enjoyed, such as good food, gardening, and the fellowship of close friends.

Tolkien held a special enjoyment for language. He loved words, and he was fascinated by the way they worked and the stories they could tell. When he was a boy, he learned several languages from his mother, including Latin. He enjoyed reading stories like *Peter Pan* and *Alice in Wonderland*, but he liked fairy stories most of all, especially the "Curdie" stories of George MacDonald and *The Red Fairy Book*, by Andrew Lang. Tolkien grew to be so interested in words that he became a philologist, a scholar who studies languages and literature. During his years of university at Oxford, Tolkien not only started writing poetry, but he invented two languages, which he said came from elves. Behind his love for language was an imagination so big, it went further than poetry or story to the realm of mythology.

Before Tolkien got very far creating his mythical world, he was summoned by the British army to fight in World War I. While serving in the muddy trenches of France, he thought more about his mythology, both to continue his creative work and to escape the bloody horror of war with his mind. Two of Tolkien's best friends also fought in the trenches, and during the Battle of the Somme they were killed. Tolkien himself was wounded by a mortar shell and had to be sent back to England, where he spent many months recovering from his injuries and other illnesses. It was in large part because of the friends he lost in the war that Tolkien was inspired to make his mythology a lifelong work.

Several other important people inspired Tolkien, including his wife, Edith (whom he called "Luthien," after an elf princess he created), his good friend and colleague C. S. Lewis, and his four children: John, Michael, Christopher, and Priscilla. Tolkien loved his children very much, and he enjoyed using his stories to entertain them. One of these stories took place "long ago in the quiet of the world," a time when elves, goblins, and dragons lived. The story was about a little person who goes on a grand adventure, and it was quite entertaining. It was so good, in fact, that it was published in 1937, and since that time, it has become a classic of children's fiction. Tolkien thought that no child ought read a book that an adult would not enjoy. And so, as you will find if you keep reading *The Hobbit*, it is a book that can both entertain and teach a person their whole life long.

## Reading Notes

| | |
|---|---|
| **Bilbo Baggins** | well-to-do hobbit living at The Hill in Hobbiton |
| **The Bagginses** | hobbit family respected for their wealth and sensibleness |
| **hobbits** | little people, half the height of humans, who relish comfort |
| **The Tooks** | hobbit family living across The Water; known for adventures |
| **Gandalf** | wizard who knew Bilbo's grandfather, the Old Took |
| **dwarves** | people of short, stout stature, with beards and a love of treasure |
| **Thorin** | important dwarf leading a band of twelve other dwarves |
| **Smaug** | dragon who stole the dwarves' home and treasure |

## Vocabulary

Write the meaning of each bold word or phrase.

1. Mr. Baggins was not quite so **prosy** as he liked to believe ________________
2. who was feeling positively **flummoxed** ________________
3. the **depredations** of dragons ________________
4. Thorin with his feet on the **fender** ________________
5. this most excellent and **audacious** hobbit ________________
6. The **estimable** Mr. Baggins ________________
7. **singed** beards ________________

## Comprehension Questions

Answer the following in complete sentences.

1. The Tooks are richer than the Bagginses, but not as respectable. Why? ________________
2. What are the dwarves planning to do? ________________
3. Gandalf says Bilbo is "as fierce as a dragon in a pinch." Why does Gandalf say this? ________________
4. Why does Gandalf choose Bilbo? ________________

5. Does Thorin have faith in Bilbo? How can you tell? ______________________________

______________________________________________________________________________

______________________________________________________________________________

## Quotations

*"I am looking for someone to share in an adventure that I am arranging, and it's very difficult to find anyone."*

Who said this? ______________________________

*"We are plain quiet folk and I have no use for adventures. Nasty disturbing uncomfortable things! Make you late for dinner!"*

Who said this? ______________________________

*"He looks more like a grocer than a burglar!"*

Who said this? ______________________________

*"Tell me what you want done, and I will try it, if I have to walk from here to the East of East and fight the wild Were-worms in the Last Desert."*

Who said this? ______________________________

## Discussion Questions

1. Explain why the second and fourth quotations show us two different sides of the speaker.
2. From where have the dwarves first come? Why did they move south?
3. Describe the glory days of the dwarves and their relationship with the men of Dale.
4. Explain the decline in the work and prestige of the dwarves as they changed from craftsmen to blacksmiths to coal miners.

## Enrichment

1. Read Thorin's story aloud in class (beginning with "O very well," and ending with "the rightful heir"). Write a one-paragraph summary of the history of the dwarves.
2. Begin filling in the Book Notes in the Appendix.

# The Dwarves' Song

1

Far over the misty mountains cold
To dungeons deep and caverns old,
We must away ere break of day,
To seek the pale enchanted gold.

2

The dwarves of yore made mighty spells,
While hammers fell like ringing bells
In places deep, where dark things sleep,
In hollow halls beneath the fells.

3

For ancient king and elvish lord
There many a gleaming golden hoard
They shaped and wrought, and light they caught
To hide in gems on hilt of sword.

4

On silver necklaces they strung
The flowering stars, on crowns they hung
The dragon-fire, in twisted wire
They meshed the light of moon and sun.

5

Far over the misty mountains cold
To dungeons deep and caverns old,
We must away ere break of day,
To claim our long-forgotten gold.

6

Goblets they carved there for themselves
And harps of gold; where no man delves
There lay they long, and many a song
Was sung unheard by men or elves.

7

The pines were roaring on the height,
The winds were moaning in the night.
The fire was red, it flaming spread;
The trees like torches blazed with light.

8

The bells were ringing in the dale
And men looked up with faces pale;
Then dragon's ire more fierce than fire
Laid low their towers and houses frail.

9

The mountain smoked beneath the moon;
The dwarves, they heard the tramp of doom.
They fled their hall to dying fall
Beneath his feet, beneath the moon.

10

Far over the misty mountains grim
To dungeons deep and caverns dim,
We must away ere break of day,
To win our harps and gold from him!

## Vocabulary

Write the meaning of each bold word or phrase.

1. We must away **ere** break of day ______
2. The dwarves of **yore** ______
3. In hollow halls beneath the **fells** ______
4. here many a gleaming golden **hoard** ______
5. They shaped and **wrought** ______
6. To hide in gems on **hilt** of sword ______

## Comprehension Questions

Answer the following in complete sentences.

1. What were the dwarves' mighty spells? ______
2. Paraphrase: "… and light they caught / to hide in gems on hilt of sword." ______
3. What item did the "dwarves of yore" make, out of what materials, and for whom? ______
4. Rewrite verses 1-3 in prose. ______

## Vocabulary

Write the meaning of each bold word or phrase.

1. **Goblets** they carved for themselves ______
2. Where no man **delves** ______

## Comprehension Questions

Answer the following in complete sentences.

1. What are "flowering stars"? "dragon-fire"? ______
2. What were the dwarves claiming besides their gold? ______
3. What do harps and goblets symbolize? ______
4. Do you think the dwarves became overconfident of their wealth? ______
5. Rewrite verses 4-6 in prose. ______

## Vocabulary

Write the meaning of each bold word or phrase.

1. The bells were ringing in the **dale** ______
2. Then dragon's **ire** more fierce than fire ______

## Comprehension Questions

Answer the following in complete sentences.

1. What happens in verses 7 & 8? Why? ______
2. What happens in verse 9? What was the "tramp of doom"? ______
3. Why did the dwarves leave their hall? What happened? ______
4. Who is "him" in the last line of verse 10? ______
5. Does dragon-fire attract dragons? ______
6. Identify the three verses in the entire poem that are nearly identical. Copy the last line of each. When read together, what story do they tell? ______
7. Rewrite verses 7-10 in prose. ______

*"... he began to feel that adventures were not so bad after all."*

## Reading Notes

**trolls** very large persons; not very clever, but dangerous and evil

## Vocabulary

Write the meaning of each bold word or phrase.

1. funeral expenses to be **defrayed** ______
2. Thinking it unnecessary to disturb your **esteemed** repose ______
3. proceeded in advance to make **requisite** preparations ______
4. parcels and **paraphernalia** ______
5. a nice bit o' fat valley **mutton** ______
6. **purloined** the beer ______
7. Gandalf tried various **incantations** ______

## Comprehension Questions

Answer the following in complete sentences.

1. What causes Bilbo to leave his hobbit hole without a pocket-handkerchief? ______
2. Where does Bilbo meet the Company of dwarves? ______
3. What is the Company's first mishap? ______
4. Where does the Company encounter the trolls? ______
5. What is Bilbo's discovery about himself? ______
6. What happens to trolls at daybreak? ______
7. What does the Company find in the trolls' lair? ______

## Quotations

*"Great Elephants! You are not at all yourself this morning—you have never dusted the mantelpiece!"*

Who said this? ______________________________

*"You will have to manage without pocket-handkerchiefs, and a good many other things, before you get to the journey's end."*

Who said this? ______________________________

*"Bother burgling and everything to do with it! I wish I was at home in my nice hole by the fire, with the kettle just beginning to sing!"*

Who said this? ______________________________

*"Blimey, Bert, look what I've copped!"*

Who said this? ______________________________

*"I am a good cook myself, and cook better than I cook, if you see what I mean."*

Who said this? ______________________________

## Discussion Questions

1. Describe what is happening in the drawing in this chapter.
2. Is Bilbo an optimist or a pessimist? Find specific phrases to support your answer.
3. Compare Thorin's and Gandalf's attempts at rescuing the dwarves. Who is successful? Why?
4. Bilbo is hired as a burglar. What are some hobbit characteristics that fit the job description?

## Enrichment

1. Add trolls to your Creature List in the Appendix. Include a description of their appearance, speech, eating habits, their natural habitat, where they had moved to and why, and what happens to them in daylight.

*"At that moment he felt more tired than he ever remembered feeling before."*

## Reading Notes

| | |
|---|---|
| **elves** | wise and noble people who are also merry and fair |
| **Glamdring** | famous elvish sword; "Foe-hammer"; belongs to Gandalf |
| **Orcrist** | another famous elvish sword; "Goblin Cleaver"; belongs to Thorin |
| **moon letters** | rune letters seen only by special moonlight |
| **Durin's Day** | first day of the dwarves' New Year, when the last autumn moon is in the sky |

## Vocabulary

Write the meaning of each bold word or phrase.

1. The **bannocks** are baking! ____________________
2. uncomfortable, **palpitating** ____________________
3. as **venerable** as a king of dwarves ____________________
4. the **remnants** of old robberies ____________________
5. **cunning** handwriting____________________
6. a bit **vexed** ____________________

## Comprehension Questions

Answer the following in complete sentences.

1. Where does the Company stop after their encounter with the trolls?____________________
2. What do the dwarves think of elves? Why?____________________
3. Describe Elrond. ____________________
4. Who is Durin? Who is his heir? ____________________
5. What does the moon's light reveal to Elrond? Write the message. ____________________

## Quotations

*"Is that The Mountain?"*

Who said this? ________________________

*"We must not miss the road, or we shall be done for."*

Who said this? ________________________

*"Hmmm! It smells like elves!"*

Who said this? ________________________

*"Stand by the grey stone when the thrush knocks, and the setting sun with the last light of Durin's Day will shine upon the key-hole."*

Who said this? ________________________

## Discussion Questions

1. In the third quotation, where is the speaker when he says this?
2. The adventure with the trolls is not an accident. What does the Company find in the trolls' lair? Where did the swords come from? How does Elrond know? Is this a foreboding that they are on the right road to their quest?

## Enrichment

1. Swords are often given names and histories in Tolkien's stories. Compose a paragraph in which you, like Elrond, tell about the name and origin of a sword of your own imagining. Draw your sword.
2. Read the explanation of runes given immediately before Chapter 1 in *The Hobbit*. Then complete the activities found in the Runic Alphabet section in the Appendix.
3. Add to your Book Notes.

*"Though he could not do everything, he could do a great deal for friends in a tight corner."*

## Reading Notes

**goblins** cruel, wicked, bad-hearted people who live underground

**The Great Goblin** the ruler of the goblins under the Misty Mountains

## Vocabulary

Write the meaning of each bold word or phrase.

1. the echoes were **uncanny** ______________________
2. the dwarves were already **yammering** and bleating ______________________
3. **ingenious** devices ______________________
4. wicked dwarves had even made **alliances** with them ______________________
5. **hordes** of angry goblins ______________________

## Comprehension Questions

Answer the following in complete sentences.

1. What is Bilbo's dream? Is he really dreaming? ______________________
2. Who are the youngest pair of dwarves? Why are they chosen as scouts? How many years younger than the other dwarves are they? ______________________
3. Why doesn't Thorin want to tell the goblin king the whole truth about their expedition? ______________________
4. How do the dwarves escape? ______________________
5. What do the goblins fear? ______________________

6. Who carries Bilbo on his back? What happens? ______________________________

______________________________

______________________________

## Quotations

*"Who are these miserable persons?"*

Who said this? ______________________________

*"We were on a journey to visit our relatives, our nephews and nieces, and first, second, and third cousins, and the other descendants of our grandfathers …"*

Who said this? ______________________________

*"He is a liar, O truly tremendous one!"*

Who said this? ______________________________

*"Why, O why did I ever bring a wretched little hobbit on a treasure hunt!"*

Who said this? ______________________________

*"Draw your sword, Thorin!"*

Who said this? ______________________________

## Discussion Questions

1. Describe the drawing in this chapter entitled "The Mountain Path."
2. The first paragraph of this chapter is a metaphor about any adventure or quest in one's life. Explain.
3. "And that was the last time that they used the ponies, packages, baggages, tools and paraphernalia that they had brought with them." To what does this sentence allude? Would they find provisions for the rest of the journey? Explain.
4. Goblins are clever but not creative. What is the purpose of their inventions?

## Enrichment

1. Copy the goblins' song in your best penmanship. Make sure you copy it perfectly. This should be copied like a poem, so that each line stands alone. Then memorize it and recite it for an audience.
2. Continue working on your Book Notes.

*"It was a turning point in his career, but he did not know it."*

## Reading Notes

**Gollum** a small slimy wicked creature living by the lake down beneath the mountain

**The Ring** a ring Gollum has possessed for many years that makes its wearer invisible

## Vocabulary

Write the meaning of each bold word or phrase.

1. **throttled** them from behind ______
2. **sheathed** his sword ______
3. **shambling** off at a great pace ______
4. he **ventured** to try ______
5. a new strength and **resolve** ______

## Comprehension Questions

Answer the following in complete sentences.

1. What does Bilbo find on the floor of the dark tunnel? ______
2. What comforts Bilbo when he finds he does not have matches to light his pipe? ______
3. What flummoxes Bilbo? ______
4. Where does Gollum live? Describe his way of life in the lake. ______
5. List some ways that hobbits are not like ordinary people. ______
6. Why does Gollum suggest a game of riddles? ______
7. Which one of Bilbo's riddles is not really a riddle? ______

8. How does Bilbo escape? ______________________________________________

______________________________________________

______________________________________________

______________________________________________

## Quotations

*"Go back? No good at all! Go sideways? Impossible! Go forward? Only thing to do! On we go!"*

Who said this? ____________________

*"Is it nice, my preciousss? Is it juicy? Is it scrumptiously crunchable?"*

Who said this? ____________________

## Discussion Questions

1. What is the speaker talking about in the second quotation?
2. In narrative form, tell about Bilbo's discovery of the ring, his encounter with Gollum, and his escape.
3. Bilbo and Gollum engage in an ancient riddle game. Can you remember these riddles? Can you make some of your own?

## Enrichment

1. Bilbo was hired by the dwarves as a "burglar" although he was given very little information about what that would involve. Has Bilbo been useful in expected ways so far? Is this how the author is showing us that he believes in Providence? Support your position in a short essay with details from the story.

*"Bilbo's reputation went up a very great deal with the dwarves after this."*

## Reading Notes

| | |
|---|---|
| **wargs** | evil wolves that live over the Edge of the Wild |
| **eagles** | proud, strong, noble-hearted birds that live in the Misty Mountains |

## Vocabulary

Write the meaning of each bold word or phrase.

1. **abominable** tunnels ______
2. He nibbled a bit of **sorrel**. ______
3. a lonely **pinnacle** of rock ______
4. eagle's **eyrie** ______
5. jumping over a **precipice** ______
6. **famished** with hunger ______

## Comprehension Questions

Answer the following in complete sentences.

1. What conversation does Bilbo overhear? ______
2. What improves Bilbo's reputation? ______
3. How does Gandalf get into the goblins' tunnel by surprise? ______
4. Where does the Company decide to spend the night? What are their misgivings? ______
5. Why are the wolves gathered near the clearing that night? Why are the goblins late? ______
6. With whom are the wargs in alliance? When? ______

7. How is the Company saved? ______________________________________________

______________________________________________

## Quotations

*"Mr. Baggins has more about him than you guess."*

Who said this? ______________________

*"A very ticklish business, it was. Touch and go!"*

Who said this? ______________________

*"Must we go any further? My toes are all bruised and bent, and my legs ache, and my stomach is wagging like an empty sack."*

Who said this? ______________________

*"I can't be always carrying burglars on my back, down tunnels and up trees! What do you think I am? A porter?"*

Who said this? ______________________

## Discussion Questions

1. Describe what is shown in the drawing located in this chapter, and tell where a person would be standing if he/she were seeing this view.
2. What about Bilbo is the speaker referring to in the first quotation?
3. Bilbo thinks he has left the dwarves under the mountains; the dwarves think that Bilbo has been left behind. Compare their different reactions to the thought of returning to the goblins' stronghold to search for their lost companions.
4. How does Gandalf settle the issue?
5. Why does Bilbo keep his ring a secret from the dwarves and Gandalf?

## Enrichment

1. The goblins' songs are meant to frighten their prey. Dwarves' and elves' songs have a different purpose. Compare and contrast their songs. What do they tell us about the nature of each race? Write your own song. Will it be a goblin song or a dwarf/elf song?

*"Now began the most dangerous part of all the journey."*

## Reading Notes

| | |
|---|---|
| **Mirkwood** | a terrible forest; the last peril before the Lonely Mountain |
| **Carrock** | a rocky island in the Great River built by Beorn |
| **Beorn** | a good man living near Mirkwood who transforms into a bear |

## Vocabulary

Write the meaning of each bold word or phrase.

1. a last **outpost** of the distant mountains ____________________
2. your present **plight** ____________________
3. paid little **heed** ____________________
4. what is left is out on the **veranda** ____________________
5. the peaks of the mountains **glowered** against the sunset ____________________
6. leaves were laid upon the **mould** ____________________

## Comprehension Questions

Answer the following in complete sentences.

1. Why is this chapter titled "Queer Lodgings"? Is there more than one? ____________________

2. Where and what is the Carrock? ____________________

3. Why does Gandalf call Beorn a "skin-changer"? ____________________

4. Why does Beorn think kindly of the dwarves? Who are Beorn's enemies? ____________________

5. What does Beorn provide for the Company's continued journey? Is this providential? ____________________

6. What is Beorn's advice about Mirkwood? Gandalf's advice? ______________________________

______________________________________________________________

______________________________________________________________

______________________________________________________________

______________________________________________________________

## Quotations

*"Don't pinch! You need not be frightened like a rabbit, even if you look rather like one. It is a fair morning with little wind. What is finer than flying?"*

Who said this? ______________________________

*"That is Mr. Baggins, a hobbit of good family and unimpeachable reputation."*

Who said this? ______________________________

*"A dozen! That's the first time I've heard eight called a dozen."*

Who said this? ______________________________

*"Be good, take care of yourselves, and DON'T LEAVE THE PATH!"*

Who said this? ______________________________

## Discussion Questions

1. Describe what is pictured in the drawing entitled "Beorn's Hall."
2. In the third quotation, what is the speaker talking about?
3. Retell Gandalf's trick of introducing the dwarves to Beorn, two by two. What is Beorn's reaction? How did he practice this same trick with Bilbo in Chapter 1? Compare the two incidents.
4. Describe the area where Beorn lives, and contrast it to Mirkwood forest.

## Enrichment

1. You should begin to see that each of the creatures, races, and places have their counterpart in the real world. Make a list of people and places you are familiar with that could be represented by hobbits, goblins, Mirkwood forest, etc.

## Reading Notes

| | |
|---|---|
| **spiders** | greatly enlarged and wicked spiders that live in Mirkwood |
| **Wood-elves** | elves who live in the home of the Elvenking in Mirkwood |

## Vocabulary

Write the meaning of each bold word or phrase.

1. trees … hung with **lichen** ____________________
2. horrible pale **bulbous** sort of eyes ____________________
3. the snapped **painter** ____________________
4. **disquieting** laughter ____________________
5. They did not care **tuppence** about the butterflies ____________________
6. the **gloaming** and the dusk ____________________

## Comprehension Questions

Answer the following in complete sentences.

1. Are the flies referred to in the chapter title literal flies? Explain. List the actual insects encountered by the Company. ____________________
2. What happens to Bombur? ____________________
3. When are the dwarves glad about Beorn's warning to them? When do they later lament the fact that they did not remember his advice? ____________________
4. What finally lures the dwarves off the path? Why and how does it happen? ____________________

5. How does Thorin disappear? ______________________________________________

______________________________________________

______________________________________________

______________________________________________

## Quotations

*"I'm always last and I don't like it. It's somebody else's turn today."*

Who said this? ______________________

*"Don't start grumbling against orders, or something bad will happen to you."*

Who said this? ______________________

*"Is there no end to this accursed forest?"*

Who said this? ______________________

*"Why ever did I wake up! I was having such beautiful dreams."*

Who said this? ______________________

*"You are no joke to carry even after weeks of short commons."*

Who said this? ______________________

*"I will give you a name and I shall call you Sting."*

Who said this? ______________________

## Discussion Questions

1. What is the speaker talking about in the last quotation, and why does he give it this name?
2. Describe the change that comes over Bilbo after his encounter with the spiders. Do you think this would have happened without the ring? Is this why Gandalf told the dwarves that Bilbo could be trusted to take care of them? Is it really the ring or is it Bilbo? Explain.
3. Because the Wood-elves elude and later capture the dwarves, they appear to be hostile. Using the description found in the chapter, summarize the characteristics of this race.

## Enrichment

1. Draw a picture of Bilbo in action with his sword.

*"At last he had the desperate beginnings of a plan."*

## Reading Notes

**The Elvenking** the king of the Wood-elves of Mirkwood; good but stern

## Vocabulary

Write the meaning of each bold word or phrase.

1. They were **surly** and angry ____________________
2. the darkest and **remotest** corners ____________________
3. **potent** wine ____________________
4. His fears were quite **justified** ____________________
5. idle **toss-pot** ____________________
6. Where the **kine** and oxen feed! ____________________
7. **shingly** shore ____________________

## Comprehension Questions

Answer the following in complete sentences.

1. The dwarves are captured by Wood-elves. What are the advantages of this mishap? ____________________
2. Why do the elves have no need of tying up their prisoners? ____________________
3. What are the crimes the dwarves are accused of committing? ____________________
4. How does Bilbo escape capture? ____________________
5. What good results from Bilbo's invisible presence in the Wood-elves' cellar? ____________________

6. How does Bilbo get possession of the guard's keys? ______________________________

______________________________

______________________________

______________________________

7. What is the weak spot in Bilbo's plan? When is this discovered? ______________________________

______________________________

______________________________

______________________________

## Quotations

*"There is no escape from my magic doors for those who are once brought inside."*

Who said this? ______________________________

*"Drat this dwarfish racket!"*

Who said this? ______________________________

*"Gandalf spoke true, as usual! A pretty fine burglar you make, it seems, when the time comes."*

Who said this? ______________________________

*"We shall be bruised and battered to pieces, and drowned too, for certain!"*

Who said this? ______________________________

## Discussion Questions

1. What plan of Bilbo's are the dwarves referring to in the last quotation?
2. Why does Gandalf leave the Company to fend for themselves? Is Bilbo living up to Gandalf's expectations? Combine information from the previous chapter with the allusions given in this chapter.

## Enrichment

1. What do you think would have happened if the Company had stayed on the path and followed all the directions given them by Beorn and Gandalf? Try rewriting this chapter with the Company remaining on the path.

*"I suppose we ought to thank our stars and Mr. Baggins."*

## Reading Notes

| | |
|---|---|
| **The Long Lake** | large lake filled by the Running River and Forest River |
| **Dale** | once-thriving town of men near the Lonely Mountain |
| **Lake-town** | town of men on the surface of the Long Lake |
| **Master** | ruler of Lake-town; a shrewd and wary man of business |

## Vocabulary

Write the meaning of each bold word or phrase.

1. the stars of the **Wain** were already twinkling ____________
2. a **promontory** of rock ____________
3. bruised and **buffeted** ____________
4. impatient at these **solemnities** ____________
5. wandering **vagabond** dwarves ____________
6. wished for no **enmity** with him ____________
7. The **quays** were thronged with hurrying feet. ____________

## Comprehension Questions

Answer the following in complete sentences.

1. Why is Bilbo's plan of escape the only route out of Mirkwood? ____________
2. Where do the barrels end their journey? ____________
3. What can still be seen along the shores of the lake when the water is low? ____________
4. Who is the first dwarf to come out of his barrel? How does Bilbo recognize him? ____________

5. Why are guards watching the bridge? Why are they not watching very carefully? ______________

______________________________________________

______________________________________________

______________________________________________

6. What do the townspeople think of the story of Thorin? ______________

______________________________________________

______________________________________________

7. What is the Master of the town thinking about the dwarves' quest? Is he sorry to see them go?

______________________________________________

______________________________________________

______________________________________________

______________________________________________

## Quotations

*"Well, are you alive or are you dead?"*

Who said this? ______________________

*"I hope I shall never smell the smell of apples again!"*

Who said this? ______________________

*"Who are you and what do you want?"*

Who said this? ______________________

*"Very well! We'll see! No treasure will come back through Mirkwood without my having something to say in the matter."*

Who said this? ______________________

## Discussion Questions

1. Describe the details pictured in the drawing of "Lake Town."
2. In the first quotation, to whom is Bilbo speaking, and why does he ask this question?
3. The men of the town are skeptical of the old legends and put on a pretense of guarding the bridge from the dragon. Is their behavior an allegory of our society's lack of faith?

## Enrichment

1. Read "The Story Behind a Name" in the Appendix and complete its exercises.

*"At last unexpectedly they found what they were seeking."*

## Reading Notes

| | |
|---|---|
| **Ravenhill** | a watchtower height on the southern spur of the mountain |
| **Front Gate** | cavernous opening at the Mountain's foot; source of Running River |
| **thrush** | large black bird that lives near the mountain |

## Vocabulary

Write the meaning of each bold word or phrase.

1. a great **spur** of the mountain ______________________
2. died away to a **plodding** gloom ______________________
3. **Desolation** of the Dragon ______________________
4. the **waning** of the year ______________________
5. alone in the **perilous** waste ______________________
6. the dragon's **marauding** feet ______________________
7. they **toiled** in parties ______________________
8. they **implored** it to move ______________________

## Comprehension Questions

Answer the following in complete sentences.

1. Why won't the men of the town accompany the dwarves to the Mountain? ______________________

2. What signs indicate that the dragon is still alive and well under the Mountain? ______________________

3. Who unexpectedly finds what they are seeking? Where and what is it? ______________________

4. What methods do the dwarves use to attempt to open the door? Why do you think they are not successful? ______________________

5. The dwarves have become dependent on Bilbo's brains and good luck. But have they begun to place blame upon him as well as praise? Summarize the conversation Bilbo overhears.

______________________________________________

______________________________________________

______________________________________________

6. What event causes Bilbo to recall the message in the runes? Explain. ______________

______________________________________________

______________________________________________

______________________________________________

## Quotations

*"Not at any rate until the songs have come true!"*

Who said this? ______________________

*"There lies all that is left of Dale."*

Who said this? ______________________

*"I am too fat for such fly-walks. I should turn dizzy and tread on my beard, and then you would be thirteen again."*

Who said this? ______________________

*"You said sitting on the doorstep and thinking would be my job …"*

Who said this? ______________________

## Discussion Questions

1. What is happening when the second quotation is said?
2. Explain the meaning of this sentence: "They were at the end of their journey, but as far as ever, it seemed, from the end of their quest."
3. What is the importance of this chapter title? Do you remember Bilbo's statement to the dwarves in Chapter 1? In this chapter, what is Bilbo's most important role?

## Enrichment

1. Tolkien is not only a great storyteller, he is also a beautiful prose writer. Copy the final paragraph of this chapter in your best penmanship, paying close attention to sentence structure and the mood Tolkien sets with his use of words. Then draw a picture based on the image you conjure up as you read this paragraph.

*"He was in grievous danger of coming under the dragon-spell."*

## Reading Notes

**Arkenstone** a great white gem; the heart of the mountain

## Vocabulary

Write the meaning of each bold word or phrase.

1. the others made no **pretence** of offering ______
2. gold **wrought** and unwrought ______
3. **cowered** down in fright. ______
4. He **issued** from the Gate ______
5. **replenish** our supplies ______
6. These don't sound so **creditable**. ______
7. Your information is **antiquated**. ______
8. his **foreboding** grew ______

## Comprehension Questions

Answer the following in complete sentences.

1. What is Bilbo's reaction to Thorin's speech? ______
2. As he sets out for the next phase of the adventure, what does Bilbo now rely upon instead of a pocket-handkerchief? ______
3. What is the bravest thing that Bilbo ever does? ______
4. What is Bilbo's first actual theft? How does this demonstrate the dwarves' unrealistic expectations of their burglar? ______

5. How is Bilbo enchanted by the dragon's talk? What does this cause him to suspect? ____________

______________________________________________________________

______________________________________________________________

______________________________________________________________

6. What is Bilbo's ploy in discovering Smaug's weak spot? ____________

______________________________________________________________

______________________________________________________________

______________________________________________________________

______________________________________________________________

## Quotations

*"Well, thief! I smell you and I feel your air."*

Who said this? ______________________

*"Never laugh at live dragons!"*

Who said this? ______________________

*"The Arkenstone! The Arkenstone!"*

Who said this? ______________________

*"They shall see me and remember who is the real King under the Mountain!"*

Who said this? ______________________

## Discussion Questions

1. To whom is the first quotation directed?
2. What is the weak point in the dwarves' plans? How does this tie in with the difference between a journey and a quest?
3. The dwarves are anxious to reclaim their treasure. What begins to happen to the dwarves as they near the dragon's hoard?

## Enrichment

1. What is the most that could be said about the dwarves? What are their best character traits? their worst? Add these to your list of dwarfish information.

## Vocabulary

Write the meaning of each bold word or phrase.

1. **cunning** devilry ______________________________
2. a little globe of **pallid** light ______________________________
3. a silver-**hafted** axe ______________________________
4. A light helm of **figured** leather ______________________________
5. the old adornments were long **mouldered** ______________________________
6. **furtive** shadows ______________________________
7. fluttering in the **draughts** ______________________________
8. In all their talk they came **perpetually** back to one thing ______________________________

## Comprehension Questions

Answer the following in complete sentences.

1. What does Bilbo mean by the expression "third time pays for all"? ______________________________

2. While searching the treasure hoard, what does Bilbo find, what does he do, and what does he say about himself? ______________________________

3. What does the mere glimpse of gold and jewels rekindle in the hearts of the dwarves? Does this urge them on through the cavern? ______________________________

4. What do the dwarves find as they seek a way out of the cavern? ______________________________

5. How many days and nights has the Company passed in the darkness of the Mountain? ______________________________

6. What is "cram"? Who describes it for us? Do we have a modern counterpart? ______________

______________________________________________

______________________________________________

______________________________________________

7. How does Balin know the way out of the Mountain? ______________________

______________________________________________

______________________________________________

## Quotations

*"While there's life there's hope!"*

Who said this? ______________________

*"Now what on earth or under it has happened?"*

Who said this? ______________________

*"It is about our turn to help, and I am quite willing to go. Anyway I expect it is safe for the moment."*

Who said this? ______________________

*"I would give a good many of these precious goblets for a drink of something cheering out of one of Beorn's wooden bowls!"*

Who said this? ______________________

*"Don't call my palace a nasty hole! You wait till it has been cleaned and redecorated!"*

Who said this? ______________________

## Discussion Questions

1. What is the speaker talking about in the second quotation?
2. Do you have an idea where Smaug is? (Refer to the last paragraph of Chapter 12.) Why is Smaug away? Does the uncertainty of Smaug's whereabouts help to prepare us for what happens next?

## Enrichment

1. Read "Inside Information" in the Appendix and complete the "Notes" section.
2. Draw the Arkenstone and copy the description of it under your drawing.

*"The thought came into his heart of the fabled treasure … lying without guard or owner."*

## Reading Notes

**Bard** a grim man; captain of the archers, descended from Lord Girion of Dale

## Vocabulary

Write the meaning of each bold word or phrase.

1. it would **quench** him ______
2. **silvered** his great wings ______
3. His last **throes** ______
4. it was **ominous** and drear ______
5. the **waxing** moon ______
6. For what fault am I to be **deposed**? ______
7. earned an **eminent** place ______
8. the Elvenking's **array** ______

## Comprehension Questions

Answer the following in complete sentences.

1. Who is the only King under the Mountain the townspeople have ever known? ______
2. Who is the grim-voiced fellow? Why aren't his companions likely to listen to his forebodings? What is his warning to the townspeople? ______
3. Why are the townspeople at first fooled by Smaug's coming? ______
4. Why does Smaug intend first to destroy the town rather than seek out and destroy the dwarves? ______
5. For what purpose does the Elvenking gather his army to march for the Mountain? ______

6. Where is the new town built? Where does Smaug fall? ______________________________

______________________________________________________________________

______________________________________________________________________

______________________________________________________________________

## Quotations

*"Perhaps the King under the Mountain is forging gold."*

Who said this? ______________________________

*"The dragon is coming or I am a fool!"*

Who said this? ______________________________

*"Look for the hollow of the left breast as he flies and turns above you!"*

Who said this? ______________________________

*"Up the Bowman, and down with Moneybags!"*

Who said this? ______________________________

*"I am the last man to undervalue Bard the Bowman."*

Who said this? ______________________________

## Discussion Questions

1. How had the information come to light in the third quotation?
2. A company of archers does not give up the fight to defend their town. Bard has spent his last arrow but one, and he is alone. What happens next?
3. In the previous chapter, the dwarves sat outside the Mountain gate wondering about Smaug's absence and noticing the gathering of birds. How is this scene connected with the battle scene in Lake-town? Where are the birds mentioned next? Why did the author write two chapters about the same period of time?

## Enrichment

1. Pretend you were a visitor in Esgaroth during Smaug's attack on Lake-town and his ensuing death. Write a letter to someone back home detailing what you have witnessed.

*"Bilbo's heart fell, both at the song and the talk."*

## Reading Notes

| | |
|---|---|
| **Roac** | chief of the great ravens of the Mountain; son of Carc |
| **Dain** | Thorin's cousin and the chief of the dwarves of the Iron Mountains |

## Vocabulary

Write the meaning of each bold word or phrase.

1. **carrion** birds__________
2. a most **decrepit** old bird __________
3. **caper** about for joy __________
4. **fortifying** the main entrance __________
5. there is matter for a **parley**__________
6. the **lust** of it was heavy on him __________
7. evil deeds should be **amended** __________
8. he has **succoured** the people__________

## Comprehension Questions

Answer the following in complete sentences.

1. What indicates to Thorin that something strange is happening? __________
2. The dwarves are not able to understand the speech of the old thrush. How is his message interpreted to them? __________
3. Describe Roac. What is the message he delivers to Thorin?__________
4. To whom does Thorin ask Roac to send messengers? Why?__________

5. How do the dwarves spend their days awaiting the arrival of the armies? ____________________
_____________________________________________________________
_____________________________________________________________

## Quotations

*"It is a hundred years and three and fifty since I came out of the egg."*

Who said this? ______________________________

*"You put your worst cause last and in the chief place."*

Who said this? ______________________________

*"I declare the Mountain besieged."*

Who said this? ______________________________

*"The whole place still stinks of dragon, and it makes me sick. And cram is beginning simply to stick in my throat."*

Who said this? ______________________________

## Discussion Questions

1. What is the cause spoken about in the second quotation?
2. Read the dwarves' song. Go back to the first song. Combine the two. Do they tell a complete story? Which verse(s) of the second song are almost identical to the first? Now that the foe in the first song is dead, what foe is referred to in the new song?
3. Do you think Bard's request for one-twelfth portion of the treasure is reasonable? Why does Thorin reject his claim? What do you think of Thorin and the dwarves? Is their behavior typical of human nature? Do you think their selfish cause will succeed? Explain.
4. Why do you think the author ends this chapter with Bilbo's discontented thoughts? Try to guess what happens next. (See the title of the next chapter for a clue.)

## Enrichment

1. Memorize the dwarves' song, and recite it to your class.

*"A hobbit in elvish armour … was something new to them."*

## Reading Notes

**Dwarf and Goblin Wars** seven-year war in which dwarves hunted goblins of the North

## Vocabulary

Write the meaning of each bold word or phrase.

1. I will be **avenged** ______
2. an old bundle of tattered **oddments** ______
3. **grievous** to bear ______
4. so far past our **sentinels** ______
5. looked more **comely** in it ______
6. here you shall be honoured and **thrice** welcome ______
7. an **escort** was provided ______
8. There is news **brewing** ______

## Comprehension Questions

Answer the following in complete sentences.

1. What is Bilbo's plan that is revealed at the beginning of Chapter 16? ______
2. Thorin is obsessed with finding the Arkenstone. Where does Bilbo have it concealed? ______
3. Do you think it is fortunate that Bombur is on night watch? Why? ______
4. Bilbo is well received into the "enemy" camp, but both armies are not willing to make peace. Why not? What changes the discussion? ______

## Quotations

*"For the Arkenstone of my father is worth more than a river of gold in itself, and to me it is beyond price."*

Who said this? ______________________________

*"Not that I venture to disagree with Thorin, may his beard grow ever longer; yet he was ever a dwarf with a stiff neck."*

Who said this? ______________________________

*"I would give a good deal for the feel of grass at my toes."*

Who said this? ______________________________

*"I have an interest in this matter—one fourteenth share, to be precise …"*

Who said this? ______________________________

*"Well done! Mr. Baggins! There is always more about you than anyone expects!"*

Who said this? ______________________________

## Discussion Questions

1. What effect upon Bilbo does the first quotation have?
2. Why do you think Gandalf is pleased with Bilbo's plan? Is this another allusion to "predestination" or Providence? Bilbo chooses to do this of his own free will, yet Gandalf has been hoping this would be his choice. How does this interplay reveal Gandalf's position as prophet/angel?

## Enrichment

1. When Bilbo first set out on this adventure, he had no desire for treasure; he longed for the simple comforts of home. When he encountered the dwarves' treasure hoard, he was influenced with the desire of dwarves. Now he willingly gives up the dwarves' greatest treasure in order to end the battle and return to the comforts of home (after giving away the Arkenstone, he dreams of bacon and eggs). Did it ever appear that Bilbo would change? Write a short essay on this theme.

## Reading Notes

| | |
|---|---|
| **Bolg of the North** | Goblin ruler whose father Dain had killed in the Goblin Wars |
| **Battle of Five Armies** | a battle of goblins and wargs against elves, men, and dwarves |

## Vocabulary

Write the meaning of each bold word or phrase.

1. I could not **forbear** to redeem ______
2. **hauberk** of steel mail ______
3. Their beards were forked and **plaited** and thrust into their belts. ______
4. upon their right **flank** ______
5. bring **reconciliation** ______
6. the **vanguard** swirled round the spur's end ______
7. a **feint** of resistance ______
8. stemmed the first **onslaught** ______

## Comprehension Questions

Answer the following in complete sentences.

1. Is it a good thing Gandalf appears for the final adventure? What is his part? ______
2. What is the Elvenking's attitude? ______
3. What is Thorin's decision after that last meeting with Bard? ______
4. Why do the dwarves, men, and elves suddenly decide they are no longer enemies? ______
5. Does Bilbo doubt their victory? Why or why not? What is the turning point of the battle? ______

6. Why do you think Thorin changes his mind about giving a portion of the treasure to Bard?

______________________________________________

______________________________________________

______________________________________________

## Quotations

*"My mind does not change with the rising and setting of a few suns."*

Who said this? ______________________

*"If you don't like my Burglar, please don't damage him."*

Who said this? ______________________

*"You all seem in league! What have you to say, you descendant of rats?"*

Who said this? ______________________

*"Is this all the service of you and your family that I was promised?"*

Who said this? ______________________

*"Long will I tarry, ere I begin this war for gold."*

Who said this? ______________________

*"The Eagles are coming!"*

Who said this? ______________________

## Discussion Questions

1. Who is the "descendant of rats" spoken to in the third quotation?
2. In the last chapter, we discussed Bilbo's choice to give up his share of the treasure. Now we are seeing Thorin's side of things. Thorin accuses Bilbo of being a burglar, but that was his job description from the beginning. Discuss the irony of this accusation. What causes Thorin to turn against Bilbo? What causes Bilbo to do what he does?

## Enrichment

1. Read aloud the descriptive passage of Thorin's dramatic entry into the war with his army. Then draw a picture of Thorin in his battle attire as he enters the fray. Write his call-to-war under your picture.

*"He wept until his eyes were red and his voice was hoarse."*

## Vocabulary

Write the meaning of each bold word or phrase.

1. the goblins' **mustering** ______
2. bore him out of the **fray** ______
3. his wrath was **redoubled** ______
4. the **trackless** dark ______
5. Victory had been **assured** ______
6. **Yule-tide** was warm ______

## Comprehension Questions

Answer the following in complete sentences.

1. Who is waiting to say farewell to Bilbo? How does their meeting end? ______
2. Who buries Thorin? What is placed on his breast? Is this a good idea? ______
3. Who places what upon Thorin's tomb? ______
4. Which dwarves have fallen in battle? How many now remain? ______
5. Who becomes king in Thorin's place? Is he a better king? Why or why not? ______
6. What does Bilbo give to the Elvenking? What is his reason? ______
7. What treasure does Bilbo carry with him? ______
8. Who begins the journey home with Bilbo? Who do they stop to visit on the way? ______

9. What happens to Bilbo? Is this good or bad, or both? ______________________________

______________________________________________________________

______________________________________________________________

## Quotations

*"This invisibility has its drawbacks after all."*

Who said this? ______________________

*"There is more in you of good than you know, child of the kindly West."*

Who said this? ______________________

*"There let it lie till the Mountain falls!"*

Who said this? ______________________

*"Farewell! O Gandalf! May you ever appear where you are most needed and least expected!"*

Who said this? ______________________

## Discussion Questions

1. What are the drawbacks of invisibility mentioned in the first quotation?

## Enrichment

1. As Bilbo's adventure comes to a close, summarize the lessons he has learned. What has he learned about dwarves? about elves? Is he wiser for his experiences? What does he now value? Has this changed? Is he now richer in character than in gold? Summarize Bilbo's reflections in a short essay.

*"You are only quite a little fellow in a wide world after all!"*

## Vocabulary

Write the meaning of each bold word or phrase.

1. **brink** of the valley ______
2. lower **glades** of the wood ______
3. masters of **lore** ______
4. Sale to **commence** at ten o'clock sharp ______
5. **Presumed** Dead ______
6. a great deal more than a **nine days' wonder** ______
7. Mr. Baggins' waistcoat was more **extensive** ______
8. Lake-town was **refounded** ______

## Comprehension Questions

Answer the following in complete sentences.

1. What business had occupied Gandalf while the Company was on its quest? ______
2. What do Bilbo and Gandalf find when they come to the place where they encountered the trolls? What does Gandalf insist, and why? ______
3. Where does Bilbo finally get a pocket-handkerchief? What meaning do you think the author intended for this little detail in the story? ______
4. What does Bilbo do to make Gandalf wonder what is the matter with him? ______
5. How does Bilbo's adventure change his habits and personality? ______

6. Who pays Bilbo an unexpected visit? From what you have gathered in the story, why does this particular dwarf come to see Bilbo? What news does he bring of Dale?____________________

## Quotations

*"Your lullaby would waken a drunken goblin!"*

Who said this? ____________________

*"And your snores would waken a stone dragon."*

Who said this? ____________________

*"My dear Bilbo! Something is the matter with you! You are not the hobbit that you were."*

Who said this? ____________________

## Discussion Questions

1. Throughout his journeys, Bilbo keeps the end in view: comfort and home. In your opinion, what would have happened to Bilbo had he arrived at Bag-End a few days too late?

## Enrichment

1. What are Gandalf's final remarks to Bilbo? How does this last conversation sum up Bilbo's experiences? Write a summary of the journey from Bilbo's viewpoint of "there and back again."
2. If you know the story of *The Odyssey*, write a comparison between these two stories.

# Appendix

# Book Notes: Dwarves

Start a list of the 13 dwarves and record their appearance as described in each chapter. As you read the book, add additional information about their personality traits and special skills. Number the dwarves as their names appear in the text.

# Book Notes: Creature List

Start a list of the different races/creatures encountered in *The Hobbit*. Describe each race or creature, giving appearance, personality, activities, homeland, etc.

1. **Hobbits**

2. **Dwarves**

3. **Wizards**

4. **Elves**

5. **Trolls**

## Spelling

1. further/farther ____________________
2. hither/thither ____________________
3. Learn these spelling demons: handkerchief, suffocated, gorgeous
4. Homophones: horde/hoard
5. Homonyms: row/row
6. Masonry terms: joint, crevice, post, lintel, threshold, bar, bolt, keyhole

Note this: dwarf / dwarves

### Give the American spellings of these British words:

clamour ____________
cosily ____________
grey ____________
armour ____________
traveller ____________
neighbour ____________
splendour ____________
parlour ____________
councillor ____________
honour ____________
marvellous ____________
humour ____________
colour ____________
favourite ____________
valour ____________
carcasse ____________

### Give meanings for these archaic words:

breeches ____________
benighted ____________
waistcoat ____________
portcullis ____________
chestnut ____________
fretted ____________
oddments ____________
furrier ____________
unbeknown ____________
mead ____________
bracken ____________
hart ____________
shirking ____________
champing ____________
fetch ____________
smote ____________
larch ____________
flagons ____________
dell ____________
quaff ____________
turnkey ____________
bidding ____________
hewn ____________
plight ____________
quest ____________
fell ____________
lade ____________
hark ____________
realm ____________
dratted ____________
fortnight ____________
throve / thriven ____________

### Tolkien words:

gnawingly hungry
hooting and hallooing
bebother
prachingly thirsty
confusticate
miserableness / miserabler

# Runic Alphabet

Figure out the Runic Alphabet by using Thror's map, Gandalf's translation of the runes in Chapter 1, and Elrond's translation in Chapter 3.

**NOTE**: The runes for "U" and "I" are used for "V" and "J."

# Runic Alphabet Translation

Translate the following two runic sentences:

ᚦᛖ·ᚻᚩᛒᛒᛁᛏ·ᚩᚱ·ᚦᛖᚱᛖ·ᚪᚾᛞ·ᛒᚪᚳᚳ·ᚪᚷᚪᛁᚾ·ᛒᛖᛁᛝ·ᚦᛖ·ᚱᛖᚳᚩᚱᛞᛋ·
ᚩᚠ·ᚪ·ᚣᛠᚱᛋ·ᛁᚩᚢᚱᚾᛖᚣ·ᛗᚪᛞᛖ·ᛒᚣ·ᛒᛁᛚᛒᚩ·ᛒᚪᚷᚷᛁᚾᛋ·ᚩᚠ·ᚻᚩᛒᛒᛁᛏᚩᚾ:

1. ______________________________

______________________________

______________________________

______________________________

ᚳᚩᛗᛈᛁᛚᛖᛞ·ᚠᚱᚩᛗ·ᚻᛁᛋ·ᛗᛖᛗᚩᛁᚱᛋ·ᛒᚣ·ᛁᚱᚱ·ᛏᚩᛚᚳᛁᛖᚾ·ᚪᚾᛞ·
ᛈᚢᛒᛚᛁᛋᚻᛖᛞ·ᛒᚣ·ᚷᛖᚩᚱᚷᛖ·ᚪᛚᛚᛖᚾ·ᚪᚾᛞ·ᚢᚾᚹᛁᚾ·ᛚᛏᛞ:

2. ______________________________

______________________________

______________________________

______________________________

Translate these inscriptions on Thror's map:

ᚠᛁᚢᛖ·ᚠᛟᛏ·ᚻᛁᚷᚻ·ᚦᛖ·ᛞᚩᚱ·ᚪᚾᛞ·ᚦᚱᛟ·ᛗᚪᚣ·ᚹᚪᛚᚳ·ᚪᛒᚱᛖᚪᛋᛏ:ᚦᚦ

3. ______________________________

______________________________

______________________________

______________________________

ᛋᛏᚪᚾᛞ·ᛒᚣ·ᚦᛖ·ᚷᚱᛖᚣ·ᛋᛏᚩᚾᛖ·ᚻᚹᛖᚾ·ᚦᛖ·ᚦᚱᚢᛋᚻ·ᚳᚾᚩᚳᚳᛋ·ᚪᚾᛞ·
ᚦᛖ·ᛋᛖᛏᛏᛁᛝ·ᛋᚢᚾ·ᚹᛁᚦ·ᚦᛖ·ᛚᚪᛋᛏ·ᛚᛁᚷᚻᛏ·ᚩᚠ·ᛞᚢᚱᛁᚾᛋ·ᛞᚪᚣ·ᚹᛁᛚᛚ·
ᛋᚻᛁᚾᛖ·ᚢᛈᚩᚾ·ᚦᛖ·ᚳᛖᚣᚻᚩᛚᛖ:

4. ______________________________

______________________________

______________________________

______________________________

# The Story Behind a Name

The author of *The Hobbit*, J. R. R. Tolkien, thought that there was more to a name than just a random combination of letters. A name has a meaning; it refers to something else. For example, when you hear or read the word *dwarf*, a picture comes into your mind. Your picture may be a little different than someone else's (e.g., a short, stout man with a long beard and stocking cap), but it is nevertheless a concept you have gotten and stored in your head. Words have meaning because they point to something we have come to know by discovering in everyday life. Of course, you have probably never seen a dwarf in person, and dwarves are not "real," in a sense, because you cannot go up to one and shake his hand. On the other hand, you know what a dwarf is because there are stories about them. The word *dwarf* means something to us because dwarves have a story—in fact, many stories. You are in the midst of reading one now, and there are other stories about dwarves you have read before or might read in the future (e.g., *Snow White and the Seven Dwarves*). Stories are what give meaning to a name like *dwarf* beyond just the sound that the letters d-w-a-r-f make when said together. In summary, a name has meaning because there's a story behind it.

One day Tolkien was reading a very old book called the *Poetic Edda*, and he came across a list of names. Although the list said little about who the people were, Tolkien knew that they must have had some meaning and significance, or else the author would not have included them. As he was pondering these names, he started to guess at the stories behind them. Take a look at the list yourself, and see what you think he came up with:

Mótsognir rose, mightiest ruler
of the kin of dwarfs, but Durin was another;
They molded many manlike bodies
—the dwarfs under earth, as Durin said.

Nýi and Nithi, 2 Northri and Suthri,
Austri and Vestri, 3 Althjóf, Dwalin,
Nár and Náin, Níping, Dáin,
Bifur, Bofur, Bombur, Nóri,
Án and Onar, Ái, Mjóthvitnir.

Veig and Gandálf, Vindálf, Thráin,
Thekk and Thorin, Thrór, Vit, and Lit,
Nár and Regin, Nýráth and Ráthsvith;
now is reckoned the roster of dwarfs.

Two dwarves from an edition of Völuspá (1895), by Lorenz Frølich

You probably recognized a few names: Dwalin, Bifur, Bofur, Bombur, Nori, Thorin, Durin (the ancestor of the dwarves), and Gandalf. As Tolkien pondered these names, he was puzzled by this last one. The last part of Gandalf, "alf," is another spelling for "elf." Tolkien knew that elves were always kept distinct from dwarves in old myths and tales. He also knew that the first part of the name, "Gand," meant "wand" or "wizard's staff." Tolkien concluded that the name "Gandalf," or "staff-elf," must have belonged to an elf-like person with magical powers, indeed, a wizard. If that was the case, asked Tolkien, then what was a wizard doing in a list of dwarves? Could it be that long ago a band of dwarves had gotten mixed in with a wizard on some adventure? That is, at least, the story Tolkien saw behind the names.

# The Story of Your Name

Your name has a story behind it. It has a meaning, a history, and it sums up a lot of information in just a few letters. When you introduce yourself to someone by giving your name, from then on that person will attach your name to a particular human being, who is different from every other human being, and who plays a unique part in the world. Your name, therefore, is important, because it's a summary of you. Answer the questions below to better understand the story of your name.

## Exercise 1

What does your name mean to others who know you? Go to someone who has known you your whole life, such as a parent, and ask them to answer the following questions about your name:

1. How was my name chosen? ______________________________

2. What does my name mean? ______________________________

## Exercise 2

Imagine that you were a person living in Middle-Earth, the ancient world where *The Hobbit* takes place. Then imagine that J. R. R. Tolkien came across your name in some old book and decided to write a story in which you were one of the characters. He would have certain questions about you, like what kind of being you were and what adventures you undertook. Answer the following questions that he might have asked when he came across your name.

1. What race is this person (e.g., dwarf, elf, wizard, hobbit, etc.)? ____________________

2. What part of Middle-Earth do they come from (e.g., Hobbiton, Mirkwood, the Misty Mountains, etc.)?

3. What adventure were they involved in? ______________________________

Have you ever watched a movie that reminded you of another story or movie? There may have been a scene or character that looked like one from another story. When one story makes an unannounced reference to another story, it is called an allusion.[1] The author will not say that he or she is alluding to something else when doing it; the reader is expected to see it without being told directly that it is there. One recent and popular example is the movie *Shrek*. There are dozens of allusions to other stories throughout this animated film. At the end of the movie, for instance, Gingy the gingerbread man says, "God bless us, everyone." If you had read or seen a version of Charles Dickens' *A Christmas Carol* before seeing this movie, when you heard this quote you would have been reminded of the little boy named Tiny Tim, who says the very same line at the end of Dickens' story. Allusions, therefore, are like echoes. An echo is not the same thing as the sound that it came from, since it is softer and less clear, but it is similar enough to the first sound to be recognized as coming from it. And so it is with allusions. The gingerbread man is not the exact same person as Tiny Tim, but they have some similarities and they say the exact same line. An allusion is not the same thing as the source from which it comes, but is recognizable to a reader who knows the source.

Tiny Tim and Bob Cratchit as depicted in the 1870s by Fred Barnard

Of course, in order to recognize an allusion, a reader has to have read its source. Remember, allusions are not spelled out for the reader. The reader is expected to already have "inside information" about the source being echoed. Many readers, including you and me, miss allusions all the time because we don't recognize their source. Just as an inside joke is not funny to those without the background knowledge, so an allusion goes over the heads of readers without prior knowledge of its source. Yet, if you have that prior knowledge, or inside information, allusions can give you a fuller, richer, and more enjoyable experience when reading. Many scenes from *Shrek* are funny to a young child because of their silly antics and fairy tale qualities, but they are even funnier to an older person who recognizes the humorous allusions they make. The reason for this is not because you have to be an adult to enjoy allusions, but that you have to be informed. The best way to be informed is to develop and grow a love for reading.

Let us practice by reading a bit from a story written long ago in England called *Beowulf*. This is a story about knights, monsters, a dragon, and especially the hero named Beowulf. It is quite an adventure, and it's a story you will do well to read in full in later years. It is such an old tale that it has become a source for many allusions in newer stories.

---

1 An *allusion* is not the same as an *illusion*. An illusion is something that deceives by appearing to be real (e.g., a magic trick).

As you read the section below, ask what story or scene from a story may be echoing this source.

And so it was that the kingship of that broad land came into Beowulf's hands, and he ruled it well for fifty winters. He was a venerable old king who protected his land, until on dark nights, one dragon began to rage. It guarded a hoard high upon a hill in a steep barrow of stone. A straight path led beneath the hill; it was seldom traveled by men. One man, however, chanced upon that cave and saw the heathen's hoard. While the watcher slept, he took in his hand a golden goblet and did not give it back. The guardian's wrath would soon make the prince and people pay for those thievish wiles! … When the dragon awoke, this new quarrel was kindled. He immediately sniffed the scent of the stone. The dark-hearted one found the footprints of that foe who had walked undetected by the creature's head … The guardian of gold went tracking over the ground, eager to find the man who had brought mischief upon his slumber. Savage and burning, he circled 'round the barrow; no man was in that wasteland. Yet he desired war and was eager for combat. He entered and sought the cup, soon discovering that a mortal had sifted through his treasure, the noble gold.

A 1908 depiction of Beowulf fighting the unnamed dragon, by J. R. Skelton

Did you notice anything familiar? Perhaps a few words rung a bell: *dragon, hoard, golden goblet/cup, thief, undetected, slumber, wasteland*. Think about these words and explain the ways that J. R. R. Tolkien alludes to this story in *The Hobbit*. You may discuss what you discover with someone else, and you may record what you find on the lines below.

## Notes: